1 Keukenhof / Inhoud
2- 3 Kinderdijk
4- 5 Amsterdam, Sail, Centraal Station
6- 7 Amsterdam, Damplein
8- 9 Amsterdam, Anne Frankhuis, Westerkerk
10-11 Amsterdam, Singel, Lutherse kerk
12-13 Amsterdam, Amstel, Stopera, Magere brug
14-15 Amsterdam, Oude Schans, Rembrandthuis, Zuiderkerk
16-17 Amsterdam, Montelbaantoren, Waag, St. Nikolaaskerk
18-19 Amsterdam, Rijksmuseum, Van Goghmuseum, Concertgebouw, Westerkerk, Stadsschouwburg, Zuiderkerk,
20-21 Amsterdam by night
22-23 Amsterdam Airport Schiphol
24-25 Keukenhof
26-27 Broek in Waterland, Monnickendam

28-29 Volendam
30-31 Marken
32-33 Noord Holland
34-37 Zaanse Schans
38-39 Alkmaar, Afsluitdijk
40-41 Enkhuizen, Hoorn
42-43 Leidschendam
44-45 Den Haag, Ridderzaal, Passage
46-47 Den Haag, Noordeinde, Huis ten Bosch
48-49 Miniatuurstad Madurodam
50-51 Scheveningen
52-53 Rotterdam, Euromast, Erasmusbrug, Shellgebouw, Nationale Nederlanden
54-55 Rotterdam, Blaak, Spaansekade
56-57 Rotterdam, Stadhuis, Delfshaven, St. Laurenskerk
58-59 Delft, Stadhuis, Nieuwekerk Oostpoort
60-61 Oudewater, Gouda
62-63 Dijk en rivier
64-67 Utrecht, Domtoren, Oudegracht, Nieuwegracht

68-69 Oude Aade, Weesp Loenen a.d. Utr. Vecht
70-71 Spakenburg, Amersfoort
72-73 Elburg, Harderwijk, Kampen
74-75 Giethoorn, Staphorst Genemuiden
76-77 Assen, Orvelte
78-79 Groningen, Martinitoren, Groningermuseum
80-81 Sneek, IJlst, Slooten, Woudsend
82-83 Arnhem, Nijmegen, 's Hertogenbosch
84-85 Breda, Biesbos, Heusden, Loevestein
86-87 Zierikzee
88-89 Middelburg, Vlissingen, Sluis, Oosterscheldekering
90-91 Venlo, Maastricht, Roermond
92-93 Thorn, Valkenburg, Margraten
94-95 Kinderdijk
96 Kinderdijk / Colofon

The village of **Kinderdijk** in the province of Zuid-Holland is the meetingpoint of the rivers "Noord" and "Lek". It is well-known for its 19 windmills, which date from 1740. They are believed to be the largest in Holland.

The Central Station of the Dutch Railways (NS). The monumental facade dates from 1889. This station was built by the harbour on one of the three artificially constructed islands. The foundations consist of 8,687 wooden piles (tree trunks). In the beautiful white building directly opposite the main entrance to the station you will find a traditional Dutch coffee house. The Tourist Information Office (VVV) can be found inside also, which offers excellent service. Every five years, Amsterdam hosts a magnificent spectacle known as "Parade of Sail". All kinds of historical ships from around the world "parade" along the IJ. This event lasts for one week and during that time swarms of sightseeing and pleasure boats weave their way between the impressive ships. On the photo to the left, the replica of the VOC ship "Amsterdam", proudly dominating the harbour. VOC stands for the "United East Indian Company".

Damplein is the main and definitely the most lively square in Amsterdam. It connects the Damrak with the Rokin. The Royal Palace on Damplein was built as a town hall in 1648. The imposing building with its neoclassic facade rests on 13,059 wooden piles. The town hall was converted into a palace in 1808 during the short rule of Louis Bonaparte, the brother of Napoleon I. The National Monument on the Dam is the liberation monument for the Netherlands, in remembrance of all who fell during the Second World War. It was completed in 1956. Since then, a memorial service is held every year at 20.00 hours on 4th May, the eve of Liberation Day. Prior to two minutes silence, wreathes are laid by Her Majesty the Queen, representatives of the government, and many others. This sea of flowers can be seen on the upper right photo.

8

The Westerkerk (upper left photo) situated at Prinsengracht 279 dates from 1620. The 85 metre tower dominates the surroundings. Building was commenced by Hendrik de Keyzer and his son completed the work with the help of Cornelus Dancker. The tower carries the crown of Maximiliaan van Oostenrijk. A memorial shield can be found in the church, due to the fact that the painter Rembrandt is buried here. However, the exact site of his grave is not known. The photo right shows 'Anne Frankhuis' (Anne Frank's house) at Prinsengracht 263. This building dates from 1635. From a window in the hidden attic, Anne could see the Westerkerk. The house is a museum and monument in remembrance of the millions of Jews killed by the Nazis. Photo below, a statue of Anne Frank on Jansplein in Utrecht.

The canals in the centre of Amsterdam form a crescent shape, both ends coming out in the river IJ. The innermost canal (the shortest half circle) is called "Singel". The photo upper right shows the "Singelsluizen" (Singel sluices), which connect with the IJ harbour. In the "Golden Age" these sluices were witnesses to the valuable merchandise brought from far countries. Today, tourists from all over the world can enjoy this wonderful view, while they are sitting on the terraces by the canals, or sailing through them.

Photo upper middle, the "Singelgracht", and the Lutheran church to the right from 1671. This church burnt to the ground in 1822, and it was rebuilt in its original style. The Lutheren Church used to be situated elsewhere in the city, and German protestants held their services there up until 1648, when the Netherlands were liberated from the Spanish-Catholic occupation. Nowadays the church is a cultural centre.

Right next to the church at Singel No. 7 you will find the narrowest house in Amsterdam, photo upper left. Taxes used to be levied according to the width of the front of the house, at the canal side. A clever individual made the front of his house only as wide as the front door. Photo lower right, the "Brouwersgracht" (Brewers canal) situated nearby and named after the old breweries. Many beautiful houseboats are moored here.

River "Amstel", after which Amsterdam was named. In 1270 a dam and sluices were built to prevent the town from being flooded. In the 14th century trading took place between Amsterdam, Hamburg and Gdansk (Poland). Photo top right shows the famous "Magere Brug" (Narrow Bridge), the most striking view of the Amstel. Lower right, the new theatre for Performing Arts "Stopera", and the new Town Hall built separately, but conveniently connected by a bridge. Close by, you will find the "Vlooienmarkt" (Flea Market), upper right. Upper left, the "Moses and Aäronkerk", originally a secret meeting place for Catholic believers shortly after the Reformation. Later it was converted into a proper church with a neoclassic facade and a baroque interior. Now only used for festivals and concerts.

Standing on the bridge of the St.Anthonie sluices (locks), photos left, you can enjoy a wonderful view of the Oude Schans, one of the widest canals in Amsterdam. In the background, the Montelbaanstoren from 1512, one of the old defense towers. It was, however, nearly a hundred years later before the tower was given its magnificent spire. These towers were part of the walls surrounding the city of Amsterdam. If you turn round on the bridge, you will be able to see the "Rembrandt House" (top centre), where the famous painter lived and worked from 1639-1658. It was here that he completed his most famous painting "The Night Watch", in the same year that his son Titus, who was to become an artist too, was born. Rembrandt could not continue living in this house because of his great financial difficulties. The house has been a museum since 1911.

The Zuiderkerk (South Church), top right, the first protestant church after the Reformation, was built by Hendrik de Keyser, who also built the Westerkerk. The building has not been used for church services since 1929. After many years of radical restoration, it is now used as an exhibition centre.

On the left, a close up of Montelbaanstoren (see also page 12). This tower dates from the 15th century, and it is one of the many towers that were part of the defence system of the city. The Elandsgracht/Waals canal (upper centre), with its beautiful, old houses, famous for their façades and gables and the St. Nicolaaskerk (St. Nicholas church) in the background. See also page 5. Lower right, the Waag (public scales building). This red masonry building, with its five towers, used to be one of the entrances to the city. Later, the Medical Guild established itself here. Reason enough for Rembrandt to paint "The Lesson of Anatomy" here. This painting is on display at the Mauritshuis in The Hague.

The Rijksmuseum (National Museum) from 1885, built in a neoclassic style by the architect P.J.H. Cuypers (upper left photo). The museum is especially well known because it houses the world's largest collection of paintings from the 15th and 17th centuries. At the back of the monumental building, in stone relief, Rembrandt can be seen working on his master-piece "De Staalmeesters" (The Sampling Officials), photo middle left. His most famous work is the 'Night Watch' from 1642. The Van Gogh Museum with its 200 paintings, 500 drawings and 700 letters from the painter Vincent van Gogh is shown in the photo left down. The collection includes the sombre paintings of The Hague and the Dutch province of Drenthe (1881-1883), and those

from Nuenen (1883-1885) in the Dutch province of Noord Brabant.
You can see self-portraits performed with the help of a mirror, the bridge of Langlois, and the yellow house in Arles. On 27 July 1890 Van Gogh attempted suicide. He died two days later in Auvers-sur-Oise. The building, dating from 1973, is a work of art by the famous Utrecht architect Gerrit Rietveld. Many more of Van Gogh's works can be seen in the Kröller Müller Museum. The Concertgebouw (Concert Hall) from 1888 is situated on the Van Baerlestraat. The photos right show the exterior and the interior during a concert. Further photos below from left to right: the Stadsschouwburg (National Theatre), the Zuiderkerk and the Westerkerk where the artist Rembrandt is buried.

Photo top left, the famous Carré theatre, originally built as a circus by Oscar Carré (1887). Photo centre left, the Royal Palace on the Dam square which is now used for representative purposes only. Photo below left, the Herengracht. Photo below right, the Central Station, built by Cuypers, with the old Dutch Coffee-house in the foreground, which houses also the Tourist Office (VVV). The large photo, top right, the well known "Magere Brug" (narrow bridge) over the river Amstel.

'Amsterdam Airport Schiphol' one of the largest and most modern airports in Europe. Passengers here have the choice of 80 airlines and 225 destinations. There is a Tourist Information Office (VVV) in the Schiphol Plaza.

The upper right photo provides a view from the esplanade which is open to visitors. Lower left photo, the entrance of Schiphol Plaza under which the railway station is situated. The airport lies about five metres below sea level. The lower right photo shows the pride of many Amsterdammers, the Amsterdam ArenA, home ground of Ajax football club.

The roof of the stadium can be opened and closed. This design is to enable the ArenA to be used for all kinds of manifestations.

Spring is the season of flowers. The huge bulb fields cover large areas of land with an incredible carpet of gorgeous colours. The tulips are grown just behind the sand dunes where, owning to the mixing of different types of soil, ideal growing conditions for tulips have developed. This breathtaking scenery can best be admired at the **Keukenhof** near Haarlem, Lisse and Hillegom, which is world-famous for its international exhibitions of tulips and many other flowers.

Broek in Waterland, photo upper left, situated 10 km to the north of Amsterdam, is a village with many flowers and wooden houses painted in light grey colours. The authentic clog maker will be happy to show you how he makes clogs by hand using traditional craftsmanship (photo lower right).

Monnickendam lies a few kilometres away with its weighing-house dating back to around 1600 (photo upper right), which has been converted into a restaurant. In the background you can see the bell tower. Monnickendam was originally a fishing village on what used to be the Zuider Zee and was especially famous for its eels.

Volendam, one of the most visited tourist spots in Holland. It is an old fishing village and all kinds of fishing boats and yachts can still be found in its harbour. Tons of eels are sold in its famous fish auction. Along the harbour there are shops that sell delicious smoked eel, which together with caviar and salmon make the most exquisite dishes. Should you not taste them for yourself? The traditional costumes of Volendam are looked upon as the most colourful and prettiest in Holland, but

unfortunately the younger generations do not wear them very often. The best time to see them is on Sunday morning as all the women go to church. If you cannot manage a visit on a Sunday, you still find ladies in their costumes in several shops. The original beauty in the photo left has her's at "Haven 132". At all shops here you can buy gifts at very reasonable prices. From this very harbour you can take a round trip to Marken, sailing across the former Zuiderzee.

Marken used to be an island, but in 1959 a dyke was built which connected it with the main-land. Although this pretty village it is not as well-known as Volendam, you should not miss it when visiting Holland. There is parking space outside the village where you must leave your car. Then you can enjoy yourself walking around this delightful village, with its quaint wooden houses, little bridges and beautiful gardens. Marken is a living monument, not a museum, and it is just as it was hundreds of years ago. Until 1932 houses were built on wooden piles so that the living quarters were raised above the ground.This construction served as protection against flooding. Outside the village, several groups of houses can be found, built on man-made hills for the same reason. After the completion in 1932 of the 32 kms. long "Afsluitdijk" flooding was no longer a problem. If you need a film for your camera, you can always buy one at Sijtje Boes' souvenir shop on the harbour, where they will be happy to supply you with anything you need.

The next three pages are devoted to the **Zaanse Schans**.

The region around the River Zaan has an illustrious history because of its shipyards and the trade arising from them. Tsar Peter the Great lived and worked here in his youth, incognito, as an ordinary worker, so he could study the art of shipbuilding. Quaint, old wooden houses and windmills from the 17th and 18th centuries were carried,"stone by stone", from the surrounding area and rebuilt here to their original state. Only six of the forty windmills belonging to this area are left. One of them,"**De Kat**", now a fully functioning paint mill, can be visited (see photo next page top right). It is actually two 17th century mills which were made up into one in the restoration of 1960. The green mill "**De Huisman**" (The Houseman) has been producing mustard since 1786 and is still doing so. The black sawmill "**De Gekroonde Poelenburg**" (The Crowned Poelenburg) dating from 1869 is still sawing timber. The mill "**De Zoeker**" (The Searcher) dating from 1672, is an oilmill. There is also a clogmaker who will make clogs for you, while you wait and a cheese making factory. Among the picturesque green houses, which are all lived in, you will find Albert Heijn's first little grocery store. Over the years it has developed into the largest chain of supermarkets in Holland and even has chain stores abroad. You can have your colourphoto taken with the mills, which is ready at the end of your walk.

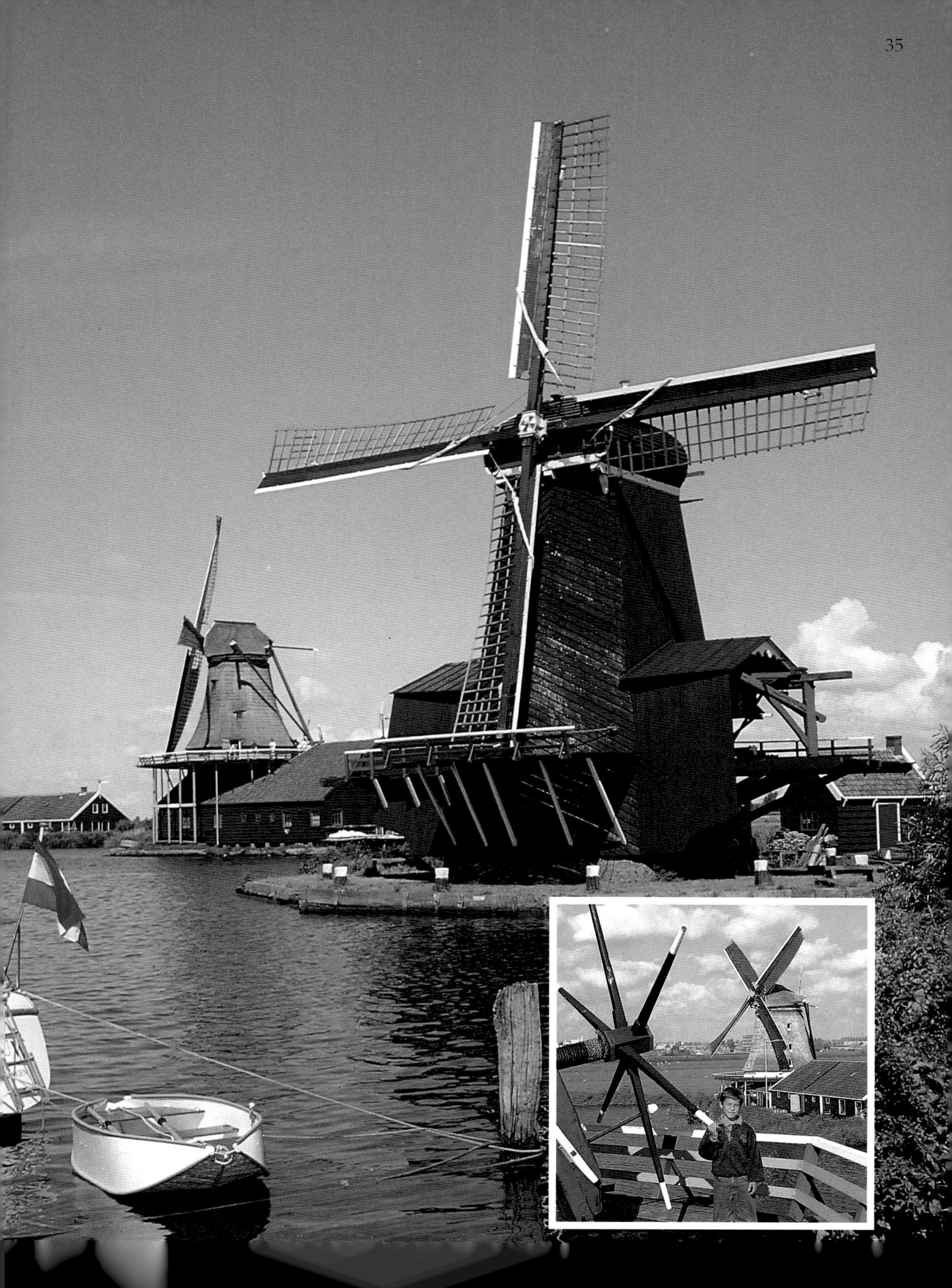

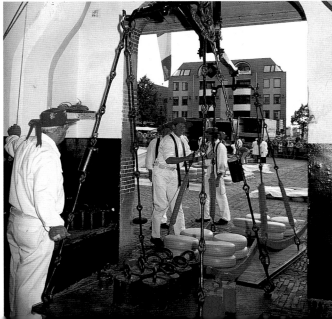

Alkmaar is rich in historical buildings. World famous is the Friday cheese market which starts at 10.00 hours during the summer. The three photos below show the inspection and trading, weighing, and conveyance of sold cheeses to the lorries. The upper left photo shows the magnificent 'waaggebouw' (weighing house) from 1582. Upper right you can see the Afsluitdijk (IJsselmeer dam). The closing ceremony was performed by Queen Wilhelmina on 28 May 1932. The dyke is 32 km long and 90 m wide, and 15 million m3 clay and 27 million kg sand were used in its construction. The dyke has transformed the old, dangerous Zuider Zee into the new, safe IJsselmeer. Some 250,000 people now live in the reclaimed land, called polders.

From the 9th century onwards, many towns were built along the coast of what was then the Zuiderzee (now called IJsselmeer). These towns flourished due to the merchant shipping on the Zuiderzee and were very important until the 18th century. Among them are Monnickendam, Edam, Medemblik and, on the photo left, **Enkhuizen** with its Dromedaris tower at the port, which is only available to pleasure boats. Nearby you find the small town of **Hoorn**, which has not lost its typical Dutch character. In this town Jan Pieterszoon Coen, Governor-General of the Dutch Colonial Empire in Indonesia was born (1620). We can see his statue in front of the Waag (public scales, from 1609). On the photo, the best known tower of Hoorn, situated at the port, which is used only as marina.

Leidschendam

Den Haag (The Hague) the seat of the government, the diplomatic centre and the capital of the Province of "Zuid Holland" (South Holland). The Hague is often mistaken for the capital of the country, which is in fact Amsterdam. Here we can see the Queen arriving at the Riderzaal (Knight's Hall) in the gilded coach where, following tradition, she opens the parliamentary year. This is a beautiful and solemn occasion, that takes place annually on the third Tuesday of September.

The Queen comes out of Noordeinde Palace (see photo following page) in her gilded coach and after a short ride arrives at the Riderzaal which is located in the Binnenhof (Inner Court). At both sides of the Riderzaal you can see the old houses of Parliament, used as such until 1992. These buildings date from around 1230. In the Binnenhof, opposite the Riderzaal, you can also see a splendid fountain, built in Neo-Gothic style. Close to this, Petra's little souvenirshop. Photo below left, the "Buitenhof" (Outer Court) with its statue of King William III and, in the background, the museum "Gevangenpoort" (Gatehouse) with, among other things, a collection of instruments of torture.

The orange pennants attached to the red, white and blue flags are symbolic of the close ties and love between the Royal Family and the people. On the photo far right you can see the Netherlands first covered shopping arcade: The Passage from 1885, which was restored to its full glory in 1991.

The Noordeinde Palace
(photo on the right) was built
in the 16th century by order
of Frederik Hendrik. Through
the centuries the palace has
been rebuilt and enlarged,
and in 1965, after a fire, it
was entirely restored. At
present it contains Queen
Beatrice's working quarters.
From this palace the Queen
goes out in her golden coach,
annually on the third Tuesday
of September, to open the
Parliamentary Year at the
Ridderzaal. On photo below,
you see the Queen and
Prince Claus leaving the
Ridderzaal, when the
ceremony is over.

The Huis ten Bosch palace (photo on the right) was also built by order of Frederik Hendrik. It is now the residence of the queen and her family. In earlier times this building used to be the seat of the governmental ministries. A famous diplomat (Johan van Oldebarnevelt, 1612) also lived here, who, later, was beheaded. Here is the Orange Room, one of the few works of baroque style in Holland.

In the miniature city of **Madurodam** in The Hague even the smallest of people feel like giants. Everything around you is constructed precisely to 1/25 of its true size.
Maduradam is a sort of synthesis of the Netherlands with many characteristic places, such as the canals of Amsterdam, the cheese market at Alkmaar, Kinderdijk's windmills, Schiphol airport, the Erasmus bridge in Rotterdam, and the Dom tower of Utrecht. There is even a burning tanker in the docks, and you can see the fire being extinguished. With so many things to be seen: you should go and have a look for yourself!

Scheveningen (photo below) the seaside resort in The Hague.
In 1982, the covered Shopping Centre "Palace Promenade", located on 15.000 square metres, was inaugurated. The 100 year old "Kurhaus" is considered one of the most comfortable and luxurious hotels in Holland. Conventions, symposiums and so on are held there. The "pier" built in 1961, renovated in the mid 1990s, offers among other things a watch tower and a big, low-budget restaurant with a magnificent view.
Upper left, the new VSB-Circustheatre in Scheveningen.
Upper right, The Hague's new Town Hall, completed in 1995.

Rotterdam, as a city has literally risen from its ashes following the devastation of its centre by bombing during the start of World War II. Nowadays it is one of the most modern cities in Holland. The port of Rotterdam has the largest freight-carrying capacity in the world. Rotterdam is the city of huge docks, commerce, hard-working people, and modern architecture. "Amsterdam has it" is the slogan of the inhabitants of the capital, and "Rotterdam already had it a long time ago" is the answer of the inhabitants of this city. The well-known Euromast tower, which is 185 metres high, is located at Parkhaven, one of the many docks on the Maas river. Via the elevator you reach the restaurant, which is 100 metres high. To go higher up you take the "space lift". From here you have impressive view of the new Erasmusbrug built by the Amsterdam architect Ben van Berkel. The bridge support is 139 m high, and the span of the bridge is 280 m. The upper middle photo shows the Hofplein with the Shell offices seen from the Hilton Hotel. Upper right photo shows the Weena Square with Rotterdam's highest office block - the insurance company "Nationale Nederlanden".

In "De Oude Haven" (Blaak/Spaanse Kade) we can see the singular architecture of Piet Blom, the cubic houses (1978/1984). Part of these fanciful houses is a bridge which connects them to the Central Library of Rotterdam. Under the bridge runs one of the busiest streets in the city. One of the cubic houses is open to the public. The building seen in the background is called (in the typical sense of humour of Rotterdam) "the pencil". The small boats at the Oude Haven (old port), and the Witte Huis (the white house), date from 1897. They show a great contrast with modern architecture.

The Rotterdam Town Hall is one of the few buildings that was not damaged by the 1940 bombings. Opposite the Town Hall we can see the attractive promenade, De Lijnbaan, with its many shops. It was built between 1951 and 1953.

Delfshaven used to be the port of Delft, but at present it is part of the city of Rotterdam. It is one of the few spots away from the hubbub of the city, and where it is peaceful and tranquil. On this little corner there is the Oude Kerk (Old Church), from where 200 years ago the "Pilgrim Fathers" left in the Mayflower bound to North America.

St. Laurenskerk, also called Grote Kerk, is a gothic church built between 1449 and 1525. It was completely destroyed in 1940 during World War II. Its restoration started in 1952 and it was completed in 1968.

Delft has a magnificent medieval Town Hall with a tower dating from 1300, of which the upper part is gothic style from the 15th century. The tower was made part of the Town Hall, which was built in 1620 by Hendrik de Keyser. It has an elaborately decorated stone façade. Opposite the Town Hall you can see the "Nieuwe Kerk" (St. Ursula), a handsome gothic church from 1384. Its belfry is second highest in Holland (after the Dom in Utrecht). The tombs of the Dutch Royal Family and Prince Willem van Oranje (William of Orange) are in this church. In the "Grote Markt" (big market), we can see the statue of Hugo Grotius (1583-1645), a talented Dutchman being a lawyer, a diplomat, a philosopher and a poet. Delft is however best known for its pottery "Delfts Blue" from the "Porceleyne Fles" (Porcelain Bottle). This skilled handwork has been produced since 1500. Photo lower left, the "Oostpoort" (Eastgate), that dates from 1400, is part of a medieval defense fortress, and it is the only remaining tower from the original eight. It owes its elegance to the two pointed towers which were built onto it in 1660, 200 years after the completion of the gate. Lower right, we can see, behind the "Nieuwe Kerk" (New Church), a picturesque little corner.

Oudewater, famous for its witches' weighbridge "Heksenwaag", and for its storks, who have a hard time every year trying to find their nests on the roof of the Town Hall. During the centuries the scales were used by the merchants to weigh their goods. The inhabitants of Oudewater, well-known for their honesty, used to weigh many people accused of witchcraft, and gave them a certificate to prove that they weighed enough. That saved a lot of lives, because if they were too light, they were accused of practising witchcraft.

When we speak about **Gouda** we think of cheese, "stroopwafels" (treacle wafers), and of candles. In the market at the triangular piazza stands the gothic Town Hall, the oldest in Holland, which dates from 1450. On its façade are some statues of the Burgundy House. The Town Hall can be visited on weekdays (excepting Wednesday). There is a cheese market in the Town Hall Square, every Thursday during the summer Still more important is the Grote Kerk, also called St. Janskerk. It is a gothic church which unfortunately is half hidden among the houses that surround it. The church is much visited for its matchless stained glass-windows of the Crabeth brothers (15-th and 16th centuries).

Utrecht is the fourth city in The Netherlands and also one of the oldest. The Romans constructed the first fortress (Castellum) here in the year 48 A.D. The canals were built between the 12th and 14th centuries.The wharves were used in the old days for unloading ships' cargoes. Goods, such as salt, wood, wine and cloth were carried to warehouses in the cellars under the houses and streets. The groundwater level fell due to the digging up of the peatbogs outside the city of Utrecht, after the water level had first reached the streets. The people living on the canals, many of them merchants, then connected their cellars to the newly constructed wharves. Nowadays, these wharves are very popular on account of their numerous cafes and cellars have been turned into attractive restaurants and little shops.

The Domtoren (Domtower), 112 metres high, and with 465 steps is considered to be the highest churchtower in the Netherlands. It commands a wonderful view over the city and the Oudegracht, photo top left. Photo left below, also the Oudegracht which meanders through the city centre. These pictures show people sitting on terraces on the wharves. The street level is above them. It could be said of Utrecht that it is a "Small Amsterdam", but more friendly.

Utrecht

Amersfoort, (right page) the second town in the province of Utrecht. On the photo we see the belfry of "Onze Lieve Vrouwetoren (Our Lady's Tower), which is 100 metres high and was built in gothic style between 1445 and 1480. According to catholic tradition, the big tower represents the Virgin Mary, and the small one attached to it, the Child Jesus "leaning" on his Mother. On the lower photo we can see the 15th century Koppelpoort, old entrance to the city of Amersfoort. To the left, **Spakenburg**, the old fishing village by the former Zuiderzee. In this village you can still see many people wearing their local costumes. Every Monday (washing day) the whole village is "decorated" with the washed clothes put out to dry on lines which go from window to window, even across the streets. In the old port (in 47 Schans Street) you will find the Spakenburg Museum, and behind the Noorderkerk (Northern Church) there is a charming exhibition of dolls, dressed up in regional costumes.

①

②

③

In 1932 the 32 km long "Afsluitdijk" dam was built across the Zuiderzee and since then it has been called IJsselmeer. Along its coast there are numerous fishing villages and lakes where all kinds of water sports are practised. Among these villages are Spakenburg, Elburg, Harderwijk and Kampen.

Elburg, an especially picturesque little town is a good example of medieval style. The old centre is completely surrounded by a canal and has a rectangular street layout. Part of the medieval town-wall is still intact.

In the 15th century Vispoort (photo 3), we can visit the Fishing Museum.

Harderwijk (photo 2) has also its own "Vispoort" from the 14th century and its wonderfully restored city wall with houses built

on it. Due to its location, near the Veluwe woods and the Veluwemeer, this town is considered an ideal holiday spot. The town is well-known because of its Dolphinarium. Along the promenade by the port (photo 1) we are able to watch how eels are smoked.

Kampen (the province of **Overijssel**), is located near the mouth of the river IJssel, became priviliged in 1230 and a hanseatic town in 1495. Until the 16th Century trade was centred around the countries of the Baltic. This influence can still be seen in the architecturel style of its various monuments. The Broederpoort (photo 4), in renaissance style is one of the three medieval town-gates. The town houses two Protestant theological Universities.

④

The west side of the province of **Overijssel** is also called "The Land of Waters". This area is located north of the city of Kampen, from which you can go to Genemuiden (lower left) by ferry boat, and from here to the "Dutch Venice", **Giethoorn.** This little village is well worth visiting. This area is also a paradise for the lovers of water sport. Its soil is rich in peat, which in old times was used as fuel. Due to the digging done to extract the peat, new lakes and canals were formed. Many of the houses have been built on islets, and you can reach them by boat or tiny bridges.

Staphorst (photo lower right) forms together with Rouveen a village stretching out over 10 kilometres. Beautiful farmhouses lie obliquely to the main street. The doors and window frames are painted bright green or blue. This is one of the few places in the Netherlands where women and girls still wear their traditional costumes.
The people do not like you to take photos of them but the lovely village is certainly worth a visit.

The province of Drenthe is also known as "The Land of Bartje". What Dutch child does not know the story of the little boy called Bartje, who once refused to say grace before his meal, saying: "I do not pray for red kidney beans!". You can see the statuette (upper left photo) of this famous little character, behind the Assen Town Hall. **Assen** is the capital of the province. Drenthe is ideal for people who want action, and for those who enjoy nature, rambling in the woods, cycling and so on. Drenthe is unique in Holland for its prehistoric tombs (lower left). These can be seen at Rolde, Borger, Anloo, Diever, Emmen, Westervelde, Odoorn, Roden and Schoonoord. In many areas of the province you are able to see flocks of sheep that by grazing help to stimulate the growth of the heather. Heather is very popular and appreciated in that area. What the tourist should not miss is the peculiar Saxon way of life of the inhabitants of **Orvelte** (lower right), near Westerbork. This village has been kept in its original state, and crafsmanship is the main feature of it.

Groningen is a university city in the province of the same name. The tower of the Martinikerk stands high above the city and can be seen from afar. The church dates from the 13th century. On the lower left photo you can see the Martinitoren from the "Martinikerkhof" (former churchyard). Photo upper left the "Kosterij" (verger's house) at the foot of the tower, seen from the "Grote Markt". Photo lower right: the Groningen museum for the city and province, which is situated opposite the railway station. Photo upper right, also on station square, shows one of the many statues in this city - "het Peerd van Ome Loeks".

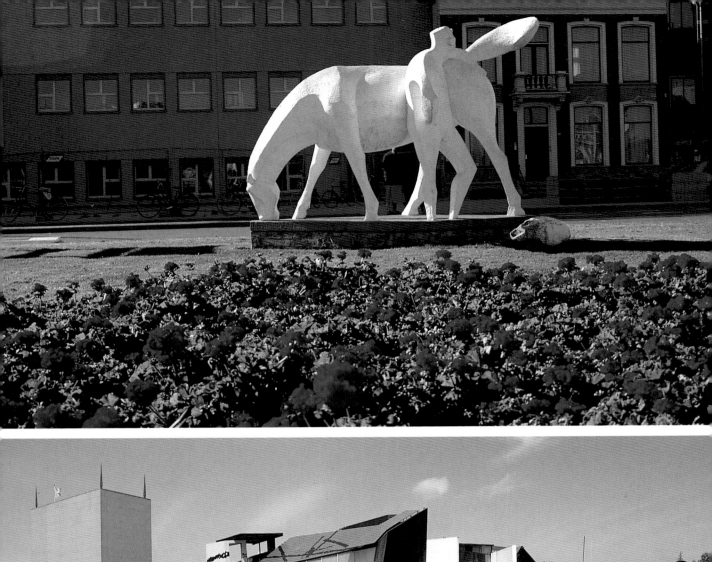

The province of **Fries-land** is famous for its watersports in the summer, such as the annual "skûtsjesilen". On the rare occasions of a very severe winter with a long period of below-zero temperatures, the "Elfstedentocht" is held. This event is a race on skates over a distance of 200 km through eleven towns or villages. "Skating fever" then rages through not only Friesland but the whole of the country! Three of these eleven towns are shown here: **Sneek** with its beautiful watergate from 1613, photo upper left; **Sloten** lower left and **IJlst** lower right. Upper right photo: **Woudsend**.

's Hertogenbosch, capital of the province of "Noord Brabant", with the interior of "St. Janskathedraal" from the end of the 14th century, photo upper left. Photo upper right: **Arnhem,** the capital of the province of "Gelderland", with the St. Walburgisbasiliek in the foreground and the St. Eusebiuskerk in the background, the immediate vicinity of the Battle of Arnhem, in 1944. Photo below: **Nijmegen** with a view of the River "Waal" and the bridge that fell safely into the hands of the allied forces during operation "Market Garden" in the autumn of 1944, in contrast to the "Bridge too far" in Arnhem.

The **Biesbosch** in the west of the province of "Noord Brabant", photo upper left, is an area with an abundance of water and marshes that came into existence in 1421. Part of it is now a protected nature sanctuary. There are also watersport opportunities and reservoirs with large reserves of drinking water for Rotterdam.

Photo lower left: where the rivers "Maas" and "Waal" converge near Gorinchem and Woudrichem, with **Slot Loevestein** (Loevestein Castle) arising in the background. To be viewed from 1 April to 31 October.

Breda, photo upper right, with the "Spanjaardsgat" (Spanish gap) through which Prince Maurits retook the city from the Spanish in 1590 by trickery (using the Breda peat barge). Now used by the Royal Military Academy.

Heusden on the "Bergse Maas", photo lower right. A beautifully and fully restored small fortified town. The streets still look just the same as they did 400 years ago.

The province of **Zeeland** has much to offer to the tourists. Since the catastrophic flood in 1953, in which nearly 2.000 people lost their lives, this part of Holland has drawn the world's attention for the impressive and vitally important engineering works, the Deltaplan. All the estuaries in Zeeland were closed by means of a barrier against storms. This barrier ensures that the population of the Delta area is kept safe and dry. New water sport areas have been formed as a result of these works, for instance Veersemeer, Grevelingenmeer and Braakman. All the delightful little villages and old towns of the province of Zeeland are witnesses to an interesting piece of history. On these pages you see two views of **Zierikzee** with its fine Town Hall chimes (16th century) on the left, and on the right the Zuidhavenpoort seen from the town. This square tower from the 15th century also has a chimes on top.

De **Oosterscheldekering** (the storm protecting barrier) on the right, is the crown of the Deltaplan. An ambitious and extremely costly project; it was a political compromise between the safety of the people and the protection of the environment. This eighth wonder of the world (as it is now called) is 2.800 metres long with 65 pillars weighing 18.000 tons each, and 62 movable steel flood gates almost 42 metres wide, part of which is immersed in the sea. The total height of the pillars is 38.75 metres. The gates are normally open, but in stormy weather or by very high water they are closed.

Photo left, **Sluis** (Zeeland Flanders) has a Town Hall that dates from 1375, with a Watch Tower that is unique in Holland. Inside the building you can see beautiful paintings from Breughel, woodcarved figurines and gobelin tapestries. Due to its proximity to Belgium, this little town is frequently visited by tourists. Its shops are open seven days a week and there are excellent restaurants and hotels.
Photo below: **Vlissingen** (Walcheren), birthplace of Admiral De Ruyter, whose statue can be found near the old port. From here you can watch the ships sailing to Antwerp or Rotterdam.

Middelburg, capital of the province of Zeeland. In 1452 the building of its Town Hall began (photo left), which is a good example of gothic style from the south of Holland. In May 1940 it was almost destroyed, but after the war it was totally restored to its original state. Also of great importance is the old abbey and its surrounding houses. This complex dates from the 9th century. The abbey has a 85 metres high tower which is open to the public. There is a market every Thursday in the Town Hall square.

Maastricht the county town of the province of Limburg. This is the oldest city of the Netherlands, which dates back to the Roman times, around 50 AD. The lower photo is of the St. Servaasbrug dating from the end of the 13th century. In the sixties, remains were discovered of the foundations of a Roman bridge some 120 m south of the current one. On the photo upper left you can see the town hall of **Venlo** with two octagonal towers, built in 1597 and restored in 1953. The city was greatly damaged during the Second World War.
Roermond with its beautiful church of Our Lady, or Munsterkerk dating from the 13th century can be seen on the photo to the right. It is a showpiece of late Romanesque style from the Rhineland area. The church was restored between 1863-1890 by the well-known architect P.J.H. Cuypers. Roermond is a garrison and is a bishop's sea.

Left, the white village of **Thorn,** an old principality, close to the Belgium border. The village square "De Wijngaard" (The Vineyard) is lined with stately white houses, its cobbled streets adorned with mosaics, and it still has gas-lighting. The Stiftskerk stands in the middle of the square and it is not only worth a visit for its beautiful interior but also for its museum of religious art.

Margraten, photo below, has the only American Military cemetery in Holland. 8.301 soldiers are buried here, 40 times, two brothers next to each other. Although the cemetery was not finished until 1960, it had been in use since 1944. The road that passes by the cemetery was constructed by the Romans, later used by Napoleon, in 1940 by the Germans, and in 1944 by the Allies. In the museum by the cemetery you can see a huge map engraved in marble that shows the military operations of World War II in Europe, and among them the one in Normandy, June 6th 1944 (D Day), and the Ardennes Offensive, December 16th 1944.

Photo upper middle, again Valkenburg with the ruins of its castle, that dates from 1040. The "Fluwelen Grot" (Velvet Cave) used to be the secret hiding place of the people from this castle.

The rivers Noord and Lek converge close to the village of **Kinderdijk** in the province of South Holland. Kinderdijk is especially well known for its 19 windmills, dating from around 1740. Not only are there more windmills here than anywhere else in the Netherlands, but they are also the biggest, and thought to be the most beautiful. They were in use up until 1950, pumping water from the polder grounds below sea level. These days their main value is for tourism. However, funded by the Ministry of Defence, the windmills are maintained in perfect working order, so they can immediately be put into use again in case of an emergency. From the inviting "Molenhoek" cafe, you can take a tour by boat. The second windmill from the cafe is open to the public for viewing.

HOLLAND,	6 talige editie	ISBN	90	5121	631	9	geb
HOLLAND,	6 talig editie	ISBN	90	5121	197	X	pb
HOLLAND, Engelse editie		**ISBN**	**90**	**5121**	**201**	**1**	**pb**
HOLLAND,	Franse editie	ISBN	90	5121	198	8	pb
HOLLAND,	Duitse editie	ISBN	90	5121	199	6	pb
HOLLAND,	Spaanse editie	ISBN	90	5121	200	3	pb
HOLLAND,	Italiaanse editie	ISBN	90	5121	202	X	pb
HOLLAND,	Japanse editie	ISBN	90	5121	203	8	pb
HOLLAND,	Russische editie	ISBN	90	5121	722	6	pb
HOLLAND,	6 talig klein	ISBN	90	5121	303	4	pb

Van dezelfde auteur verscheen eerder:
Also published by the same author:

AMSTERDAM,	Engelse editie	ISBN	90	5121	691	2	pb
AMSTERDAM,	Franse editie	ISBN	90	5121	692	0	pb
AMSTERDAM,	Duitse editie	ISBN	90	5121	693	9	pb
AMSTERDAM,	Spaanse editie	ISBN	90	5121	694	7	pb
AMSTERDAM,	Italiaanse editie	ISBN	90	5121	695	5	pb

PRINTED IN CEE

CIP gegevens.

Copyright: **bert van loo produkties bv**
Distelvlinderberm 14, 3994 WC Houten, HOLLAND
Phone: + 31 (0)30 - 63 77 301
Fax: + 31 (0)30 - 63 50 375
Chamber of Commerce UTRECHT: 30063339

Translation by Helen Dupuis - Landreth.